AGING WELL

FINISHING WELL

PETER MENCONI

MT. SAGE PUBLISHING

Mt. Sage Publishing
Centennial, CO 80122

Scriptures taken from the Holy Bible, New International Version®, NIV®. Copyright © 1973, 1978, 1984, 2011 by Biblica, Inc.™ Used by permission of Zondervan. All rights reserved worldwide. www.zondervan.com The "NIV" and "New International Version" are trademarks registered in the United States Patent and Trademark Office by Biblica, Inc.™

TABLE OF CONTENTS

ABOUT THE CASA NETWORK

In 1983, three Southern California churches established the CASA Network ministry to serve their 50+ members through cooperative efforts. The first jointly sponsored one day event was called Jamboree (now Life Celebration). The response to this first event led to a three day retreat held at a Christian conference center. A committee representing various churches met the next year to discover how to meet the growing needs of the Christian adult senior community and to discuss incorporating. They determined that the name of the new organization would be called CASA, Christian Association of Senior Adults.

In 1993 the CASA Board of Directors caught the vision to broaden its ministry to mid and post career age men and women nationally and internationally. In the fall of 1994, CASA launched two quarterly publications – The Energizer for senior adults and Energizing Leaders for leaders of Adults 50+ in the local church. With the explosion of the Boomer generation, a third quarterly publication was launched in 2001 for this population, called Legacy Living. For a time, CASA engaged in a website partnership with Christianity Today.

From 1993 through 1998 regional leadership training conferences were offered to pastors and lay leaders of adult 50+ ministries in a number of states and Canada. In 1998, the first National Leadership Training Conference was held in Irvine, CA and brought together over 300 pastors and lay leaders from 26 states and Canada. A further development in the growth of CASA's ministry was the establishment of a website **www.gocasa.org** that provides resources and information on 50+ ministry. Serving leaders across the country, the CASA Network offers regional, national, and international 50+ leadership conferences. You can access the CASA Network website at **www.gocasa.org** for the latest information on training offerings.

Today, the CASA Network is a premier training and equipping source for the Church's ministry to midlife and beyond age men and women. Augmented by internet and print media, the CASA Network brings together an array of leaders within the field of 50+ ministry to inspire and equip the Church for ministry to and through adults in life's second half. Only God knows how many lives have been touched, how many churches have been changed, how many leaders have been trained because of the vision and leadership of the CASA Network. Check us out at **www.gocasa.org** and welcome to the CASA Network Aging Well Bible Study Series.

BEFORE YOU BEGIN!
Instructions on how to get the most out of this book.

The primary purpose of this Bible study is to help you to take a closer look at how you can finish well before your life is over.

This book contains six Bible study sessions on the topics of finishing well that can be done individually or in a small group. The studies are written for people who have never studied the Bible, occasionally study the Bible, or often study the Bible. That is, virtually everyone interested in aging will benefit from these studies. Each session allows the Bible to speak to where you are and where God may want you to go.

While these studies can be done individually, they are primarily designed to be done in a small group setting. In fact, you will receive maximum benefit when the study is discussed in a group. The more diverse your group is in age and experience, the more you will learn from these studies.

SUGGESTIONS ON FORMING A GROUP

1. Form a group that has between eight and 15 members. Groups larger or smaller are generally less effective.

2. One person should be appointed as the group facilitator. The facilitator's primary role is to get everyone together at an appointed time and place. The facilitator also gets the study started and keeps it going without getting off track. After the initial meeting the facilitator role can rotate within the group.

3. At the first meeting have the group members introduce themselves to one another and have each person share his or her responses to the following questions:

  a) Where were you born and raised?

b) Where were you and what were you doing at age 10? Age 18? Age 25?

c) What one person, place, or experience has had the greatest impact on your life and why?

4. Before starting the study group members should agree on the length and frequency of meeting times. Normally, each study should take about one hour. All group members should commit themselves to attending all group sessions, unless there are circumstances beyond their control.

5. Give time for the small group to gel. Don't expect everything to click in the first session or two.

Because the interaction in a small group can reach into personal areas, it is important that group members agree upon "ground rules."

SUGGESTED GROUND RULES FOR SMALL GROUP STUDY

1. Jesus said that "the Holy Spirit, whom the Father will send in my name, will teach you all things and will remind you of everything I said to you." With this in mind, each group session should open in prayer asking the Holy Spirit to teach and guide. (Not everyone needs to pray. If a person is uncomfortable praying in public, he or she should be given freedom to remain silent.)

2. No one or two persons should dominate the discussion time. All group members should have an equal opportunity to express their thoughts, feelings, and experiences.

3. Because people's experiences and perspectives vary, there will be ideas, thoughts, and feelings expressed which will be quite diverse. All members should respect one another's perspective.

4. Confidentiality on what is said in the study should be agreed upon by all group members.

5. If significant conflict arises between specific group members, they should make every effort to resolve this conflict apart from group time. That is, they should agree to meet together at another time to discuss their differences.

6. If the group ends in prayer, members should pray for one another.

SESSION 1 | EMBRACING THE CHALLENGE

INTRODUCTION
Have one or more group members read the introduction aloud.

The Issue: What is your attitude toward aging and how can you make it better than it is?

Many years ago Bette Davis is quoted as saying, "Old age ain't for sissies." It's still true. Aging is a challenge for many people. Yet aging and older age can be a very enjoyable and productive time. There are many examples of older people being creative and growing as they age.

Helen Keller, who was both blind and deaf, started working on a new book *Teacher* at the age of 73. George Burns, the famous co-median, continued to work well into his 90s. At the age of 83, John Wesley was still writing books and sermons daily and at 86, still preaching twice a day. Miguel Cervantes wrote *Don Quixote* when he was almost 70. John Milton wrote *Paradise Regained* when he was 63. Benjamin Franklin helped to frame the U.S. Constitution at age 81. Michelangelo was in his late 80s when he painted some of his masterpieces. Thomas Edison still worked in his laboratory at 83. Dr. Michael DeBakey was still performing surgery at 90.

You get the point. Aging is not the end of life, but a time of new op-portunity. As C. S. Lewis said, "You are never too old to set another goal or to dream a new dream." How you experience your later years will greatly depend on whether you fight or embrace aging.

Research shows that how you perceive aging affects how long you will live. It is not known for sure why a positive attitude leads to longer life. Researchers offer several possible explanations. A posi-tive attitude toward aging may increase a person's will to live, mak-ing him or her more resilient to illness and more proactive about health. Another possible explanation for greater longevity in posi-tive people is that they have lower levels of mental stress.

When he was 92 years of age, Billy Graham offered some words of wisdom on aging in an interview with *Christianity Today*. Graham stated, "God has a reason for keeping us here (even if we don't always understand it), and we need to recover the Bible's understanding of life and longevity as gifts from God—and therefore as something good." He added, "Several times the Bible mentions people who died 'at a good old age'—an interesting phrase. So part of my advice is to learn to be content and that only comes as we accept each day as a gift from God and commit it into his hands."

As followers of Jesus Christ, we should embrace the second half of life as a God-given stage that presents unique ministry opportunities. Our life experiences and insights give us valuable assets in helping to further God's kingdom. This is especially true when we consider the powerful influence we can have in the lives of younger people. As we age, we can take advantage of the many creative opportunities that exist for us to reinvent and reinvest ourselves in the work of God.

YOUR TAKE
From the following list, check the responses that best answers the questions. Discuss your responses with your group.

1. Which of the following words best describes your feelings about aging? Please explain why you answered as you did.

__ uneasy	__ annoyed	__ positive
__ confident	__ angry	__ negative
__ optimistic	__ concerned	__ troubled
__ eager	__ prepared	__ peaceful

2. Which of the following statements best describes how you want to age?

__ I want to stay physically fit and active.

__ I want to be a wiser person, even a sage.

__ I want to have enough money and time to travel.

__ I want to keep working at a meaningful job.

__ I want to develop my spiritual life to the fullest.

__ I want to return to school.

__ I want to invest more time in my family and friends.

__ I want to get more involved in politics.

__ Other _____.

YOUR REFLECTION

Read the following passages from the Bible and answer the questions that follow.

Abraham was visited by three men who brought him and Sarah, his wife, surprising news.

"Where is your wife Sarah?" they asked him.

"There, in the tent," he said.

Then one of them said, "I will surely return to you about this time next year, and Sarah your wife will have a son."

Now Sarah was listening at the entrance to the tent, which was behind him. Abraham and Sarah were already very old, and Sarah was past the age of childbearing. So Sarah laughed to herself as she thought, "After I am worn out and my lord is old, will I now have this pleasure?"

Then the Lord said to Abraham, "Why did Sarah laugh and say, 'Will I really have a child, now that I am old?' Is anything too hard for the Lord? I will return to you at the appointed time next year, and Sarah will have a son."

Sarah was afraid, so she lied and said, "I did not laugh."

But he said, "Yes, you did laugh."
—Genesis 18: 9-15

1. Why do you think God waited until Abraham and Sarah were old to give them a child?

2. Do you think God waits until older age to give us certain gifts? If so, please explain your response.

3. If you were Sarah, how do you think you would respond? Why would you respond this way?

Now the LORD was gracious to Sarah as he had said, and the LORD did for Sarah what he had promised. Sarah became pregnant and bore a son to Abraham in his old age, at the very time God had promised him. Abraham gave the name Isaac to the son Sarah bore him. When his son Isaac was eight days old, Abraham circumcised him, as God commanded him. Abraham was a hundred years old when his son Isaac was born to him.

Sarah said, "God has brought me laughter, and everyone who hears about this will laugh with me." And she added, "Who would have said to Abraham that Sarah would nurse children? Yet I have borne him a son in his old age."
—*Genesis 21: 1-7*

4. How did God turn Sarah's sarcastic laughter into laughter of joy?

5. In what ways are you trusting or not trusting God as you age?

6. What "new birth" does God want to give you as you age?

YOUR APPLICATION
During the coming week think about the following questions.

1. Revisit your attitude toward aging (use the check list below as an aid). Spend some time reflecting on why you hold theses attitudes.

__ uneasy	__ annoyed
__ positive	__ confident
__ angry	__ negative
__ optimistic	__ concerned
__ troubled	__ eager
__ prepared	__ peaceful

2. Do you think God has something special for you to experience in older age? If not, why not? If so, what do you think it is?

3. How do you think God wants you to embrace aging?

SESSION 2 | ON PURPOSE

INTRODUCTION

Have one or more group members read the introduction aloud.

The Issue: As you age, what is your purpose in life and does it need to be revised?

Most of us have heard the classic story about the successful, high powered executive who retires, is lost without work and its identity, and is dead within a year. Both research and antidotal tales underscore the importance of having meaning and purpose in one's life, especially when navigating transitions like retirement and aging.

In the book *The Blue Zone*, author Dan Buettner traveled to four regions of the world (Sardinia, Italy; Okinawa, Japan; Loma Linda, California; and the Nicoya Peninsula, Costa Rica), where people generally live longer, to glean lessons on longevity. The lessons and strategies he observed and wrote about can help us to focus our daily purpose as we age. The following is a brief summary of some of the lessons that can help you create your own Blue Zone:

- **Inconvenience yourself:** By making life a little tougher, you can easily add more activity to your day.
- **Have fun. Keep moving. Walk:** Make your lifestyle active.
- **Make a date:** Getting out and about can be more fun with other people.
- **Eat better:** Information on better eating habits is ubiquitous.
- **Make relationships a priority:** Be intentional about your relationships with family and friends.
- **Create a personal mission statement:** Find an overarching purpose for your life.

For followers of Jesus Christ, our mission statement has already been written. Jesus gave it to us when he said, " 'Love the Lord your God with all your heart and with all your soul and with all your mind.' This is the first and greatest commandment. And the second is like it: 'Love your neighbor as yourself.' All the Law and the Prophets hang on these two commandments."

As we age, these words should direct the actions of our lives. Above all, the gospel of Jesus Christ calls us to be lovers...of God and our fellow man/woman. The apostle John gave us clear direction on the place of God's love in our lives. *"For this is the message you heard from the beginning: We should love one another."* He goes on to tell us that love is practical and active and not just an emotion. *"This is how we know what love is: Jesus Christ laid down his life for us. And we ought to lay down our lives for our brothers and sisters. If anyone has material possessions and sees a brother or sister in need but has no pity on them, how can the love of God be in that person? Dear children, let us not love with words or speech but with actions and in truth."*

No matter how many days of life God chooses to give us, we are to be about his purposes. Our prayer and purpose should be to see God's kingdom come and his will to be done, on earth and in our lives, as it is in heaven.

YOUR TAKE

Read the following quotations about purpose. Which ones do you agree with and which ones do you not. Discuss your responses with your group.

___ *The secret of man's being is not only to live but to have something to live for.* —Fyodor Dostoyevsky

___ *Figuring out who you are is the whole point of the human experience.* —Anna Quindlen

___ *The human soul, the world, the universe are laboring on to their magnificent consummation. We are not fashioned...marvelously for naught.* —Ralph Waldo Emerson

___ *Man's main task is to give birth to himself, to become what he potentially is. The most important product of his effort is his own personality.* —Erich Fromm

__ *Man's only legitimate end in life is to finish God's work—to bring to full growth the capacities and talents implanted in us.*
—Eric Hoffer

__ *I still believe that standing up for the truth of God is the greatest thing in the world. This is the end of life. The end of life is not to be happy. The end of life is not to achieve pleasure and avoid pain. The end of life is to do the will of God, come what may.*
—Martin Luther King

__ *Until he has been part of a cause larger than himself, no man is truly whole.* —Richard Nixon

YOUR REFLECTION

Read the following passages from the Bible and answer the questions that follow.

The boy Samuel ministered before the Lord under Eli. In those days the word of the Lord was rare; there were not many visions.

One night Eli, whose eyes were becoming so weak that he could barely see, was lying down in his usual place. The lamp of God had not yet gone out, and Samuel was lying down in the house of the Lord, where the ark of God was. Then the Lord called Samuel.

Samuel answered, "Here I am." And he ran to Eli and said, "Here I am; you called me."

But Eli said, "I did not call; go back and lie down." So he went and lay down.
Again the Lord called, "Samuel!" And Samuel got up and went to Eli and said, "Here I am; you called me."

"My son," Eli said, "I did not call; go back and lie down."

Now Samuel did not yet know the Lord: The word of the Lord had not yet been revealed to him.

A third time the Lord called, "Samuel!" And Samuel got up and went to Eli and said, "Here I am; you called me."

Then Eli realized that the Lord was calling the boy. So Eli told Samuel, "Go and lie down, and if he calls you, say, 'Speak, Lord, for your servant is listening.'" So Samuel went and lay down in his place.

The Lord came and stood there, calling as at the other times, "Samuel! Samuel!"

Then Samuel said, "Speak, for your servant is listening."
—1 Samuel 3: 1-10

1. What important role did the elder Eli play in young Samuel's life? Why was Eli able to give Samuel the directions he did?

2. Do you think it is unusual for God to call people for special purposes? Please explain your response.

3. Has God ever called you to do something specific and purposeful with your life? If so, how did it happen and what was/is the result?

For it is by grace you have been saved, through faith—and this is not from yourselves, it is the gift of God—not by works, so that no one can

boast. For we are God's handiwork, created in Christ Jesus to do good works, which God prepared in advance for us to do.
—*Ephesians 2:8-10*

Note: These verses are important in understanding that salvation through Jesus Christ is a gracious, free gift that is accepted by faith. We are saved by faith, and not by works. But as we understand God's love and grace, we are motivated to please him and do his work. God has uniquely made each of us and has given each of us unique work to further his kingdom.

4. How do you understand the salvation offered in Jesus Christ? How has this salvation impacted your life?

5. A growing relationship with Jesus Christ should be transformational. In what ways has your relationship with Jesus Christ changed the ways you live your life?

6. In what ways has your relationship with Jesus given your life purpose?

YOUR APPLICATION
During the coming week think about and act on the following questions.

1. As you age, has your life taken on a different purpose? If so, how would you describe this change?

2. Have you ever written a mission or purpose statement for your life? If so, how well does your life coincide with your mission statement?

3. Spend some time reflecting on the purpose for your remaining years. Write down specific ways you want to live a more purposeful life. Start living more "on purpose" today!

SESSION 3 | STAYING IN THE GAME

▌ INTRODUCTION
▌ Have one or more group members read the introduction
▌ aloud.

The Issue: As older adults, should we fade into the sunset or should we stay in the game to have an impact on others, especially younger people?

Many of us fantasize about the day we will retire from working. We may first worry about how we will financially be able to retire. If we adequately solve the financial puzzle, we are faced with the question of what we will do in retirement.

Perhaps, like the characters in the movie *The Bucket List,* you want to skydive or ride motorcycles on the Great Wall. Perhaps your desires are more sedate. What is on your bucket list...things to do before you die or "kick the bucket?" Research shows that the majority of pre-retirees have not clearly thought through what they will do when they stop working. Most people can give vague responses that when they have more time, they will travel, spend more time with their family, or develop hobbies.

More than previous generations, Boomers will want to stay in the game as long as possible. Some Boomers will continue working either part-time or full-time because they have to or want to. Others will travel, return to school, golf or develop hobbies. What you do in retirement should be given considerable thought long before you get there. In fact, your retirement years should be an extension of the lifestyle, values, and ideals you embraced during your working years.

For followers of Jesus Christ, staying in the game should be a given. Jesus and the Bible never talked about retirement or stopping our journey of faith. If the gospel motivates us in our current lifestyle, it should motivate us during our retirement and older years. There is no "fading into the sunset" for Christ followers. Instead, a careful consideration of how we want to spend our retirement years is in order.

There are numerous biblical examples of people God called to stay in the game. Abraham and Sarah continued to walk by faith well into old age. Moses gave God numerous excuses why he wasn't the one to lead the Israelites out of Egypt. Yet, he stayed in the game. Jonah was given a mission by God but tried to escape staying in the game. After a rough ride, Jonah finally followed through on his calling. King David continued to serve God through many ups and downs until his death. The apostle Paul tenaciously proclaimed the gospel despite being attacked, jailed, shipwrecked, and through many other setbacks. Even Jesus, in the Garden of Gethsemane, had to stay in the game to face the horror of the cross.

Our calling to follow and serve Jesus Christ is no less significant. God chooses to work through his children and this requires us to stay in the game. And each of our roles in the kingdom of God is unique. Ephesians 2: 10 tells us that "we are God's handiwork, created in Christ Jesus to do good works, which God prepared in advance for us to do."

As we age, staying engaged in meaningful and purposeful activities becomes more difficult. We may feel more physically tired. Or we may be aware that years of working and responsibility have burned us out and now feel like we have little to give. Still yet, we may become disoriented and adrift without previous structures that kept us going.

Certainly, staying in the game as we age is harder. But God calls us to make the effort. He is not done with us yet and does not want to see us fade away until we die. When it comes to serving God, we are called to flame out, not rust out.

YOUR TAKE

Answer the questions that follow. Discuss your responses with your group.

1. Which of the following would be on your bucket list?

__ Learn a new language

__ Go back to school

__ Travel to Italy

__ Complete your will and estate planning

__ Write a book

__ Spend more time your with family

__ Lose weight

__ Get more involved in ministry

__ Start your own business

__ Take up acting

__ Learn to paint

__ Do more gardening

__ Spend more time with friends

__ Eat, drink, and be merry

__ Take a cruise

__ Take music lessons

__ Volunteer more

__ Learn a new language

__ Exercise more

__ Sky dive or bungee jump

__ Learn a new hobby

__ Take a cooking class

__ Mentor younger people

__ Travel to exotic places

__ Buy a new sports car

__ Play more golf

__ Move to a warm climate

__ Work on your investments

__ Travel the U.S. in an RV

__ Other _____

2. On the following scale, with 1 being "I'm out of here!" to 10 being "I definitely want to stay in the game and have an impact," how would you rate your attitude about staying in the game as you age? Why did you answer as you did?

| 1 | 2 | 3 | 4 | 5 | 6 | 7 | 8 | 9 | 10 |

YOUR REFLECTION
Read the following passages from the Bible and answer the questions that follow.

Now faith is confidence in what we hope for and assurance about what we do not see. This is what the ancients were commended for.

By faith we understand that the universe was formed at God's command, so that what is seen was not made out of what was visible.

By faith Abel brought God a better offering than Cain did. By faith he was commended as righteous, when God spoke well of his offerings. And by faith Abel still speaks, even though he is dead.

By faith Enoch was taken from this life, so that he did not experience death: "He could not be found, because God had taken him away." For before he was taken, he was commended as one who pleased God. And without faith it is impossible to please God, because anyone who comes to him must believe that he exists and that he rewards those who earnestly seek him.

By faith Noah, when warned about things not yet seen, in holy fear built an ark to save his family. By his faith he condemned the world and became heir of the righteousness that is in keeping with faith.

By faith Abraham, when called to go to a place he would later receive as his inheritance, obeyed and went, even though he did not know where he was going. By faith he made his home in the promised land like a stranger in a foreign country; he lived in tents, as did Isaac and Jacob, who were heirs with him of the same promise. For he was looking forward to the city with foundations, whose architect and builder is God. And by faith even Sarah, who was past childbearing age, was enabled to bear children because she considered him faithful who had made the promise. And so from this one man, and he as good as dead, came descendants as numerous as the stars in the sky and as countless as the sand on the seashore.

All these people were still living by faith when they died. They did not receive the things promised; they only saw them and welcomed them from a distance, admitting that they were foreigners and strangers on earth. People who say such things show that they are looking for a country of their own. If they had been thinking of the country they had left, they would have had opportunity to return. Instead, they were longing for a better country—a heavenly one. Therefore God is not ashamed to be called their God, for he has prepared a city for them.

By faith Abraham, when God tested him, offered Isaac as a sacrifice. He who had embraced the promises was about to sacrifice his one and only son, even though God had said to him, "It is through Isaac that your offspring will be reckoned." Abraham reasoned that God could even raise the dead, and so in a manner of speaking he did receive Isaac back from death.

By faith Isaac blessed Jacob and Esau in regard to their future.

By faith Jacob, when he was dying, blessed each of Joseph's sons, and worshiped as he leaned on the top of his staff.

By faith Joseph, when his end was near, spoke about the exodus of the Israelites from Egypt and gave instructions concerning the burial of his bones.

By faith Moses' parents hid him for three months after he was born, because they saw he was no ordinary child, and they were not afraid of the king's edict.

By faith Moses, when he had grown up, refused to be known as the son of Pharaoh's daughter. He chose to be mistreated along with the people of God rather than to enjoy the fleeting pleasures of sin. He regarded disgrace for the sake of Christ as of greater value than the treasures of Egypt, because he was looking ahead to his reward. By faith he left Egypt, not fearing the king's anger; he persevered because he saw him who is invisible. By faith he kept the Passover and the application of blood, so that the destroyer of the firstborn would not touch the firstborn of Israel.

By faith the people passed through the Red Sea as on dry land; but when the Egyptians tried to do so, they were drowned.

By faith the walls of Jericho fell, after the army had marched around them for seven days.

By faith the prostitute Rahab, because she welcomed the spies, was not killed with those who were disobedient.

And what more shall I say? I do not have time to tell about Gideon, Barak, Samson and Jephthah, about David and Samuel and the prophets, who through faith conquered kingdoms, administered justice, and gained what was promised; who shut the mouths of lions, quenched the fury of the flames, and escaped the edge of the sword; whose weakness was turned to strength; and who became powerful in battle and routed foreign armies. Women received back their dead, raised to life again. There were others who were tortured, refusing to be released so that they might gain an even better resurrection. Some faced jeers and flogging, and even chains and imprisonment. They were put to death by stoning; they were sawed in two; they were killed by the sword. They went about in sheepskins and goatskins, destitute, persecuted and mistreated—the world was not worthy of them. They wandered in deserts and mountains, living in caves and in holes in the ground.

These were all commended for their faith, yet none of them received what had been promised, since God had planned something better for us so that only together with us would they be made perfect.
—Hebrews 11

1. With which of the biblical characters do you most identify?

2. What role does faith play in staying in the game?

3. God used each these biblical characters to bring his kingdom to earth. Is this fair of God to do this? If so, why? If not, why not?

4. Do the difficulties many of these biblical characters encountered deter you from staying in the game and following God's lead in your life? Please explain.

5. Why is an eternal or heavenly perspective necessary for us to endure to the end of life?

6. As you age, what is it going to take for you to stay in the game? What do you need to ask God for to help you stay in the game and do his will?

YOUR APPLICATION

During the coming week think about and act on the following. During the coming week think about and complete the following exercise.

1. Take a piece of blank paper or use your computer. Write the following headings at the top of the paper: physical, intellectual, emotional, relational, and spiritual. Under each heading, make a list of the thoughts and activities that will be necessary in each area of your life to help you stay in the game and have an impact for God's kingdom. You might include what you need to do during your remaining working years and/or what you will do in retirement.

2. Pray over your list and ask God for wisdom on how to proceed. Review your list and begin to think about and act on the next steps it will take for you to accomplish your list.

SESSION 4 | AGING IN PLACE

INTRODUCTION
Have one or more group members read the introduction aloud.

The Issue: As we age, where will we live and does it really matter?

Real estate brokers are fond of saying that the worth of a place is based on "location, location, location." Today, we have made "place" a commodity. In scripture, place and the sense of place has always been more important than that to God. Throughout the Old Testament, the spiritual health of the nation of Israel was often tied to the well being of the land God had given them. For example, when God's judgment fell upon the Israelites, he chose to punish them by exiling them from the Promised Land.

As we read the Bible, we often do not comprehend and apprehend the important role of place in God's story of redemption. From the very beginning in the Garden of Eden to the revelation of the New Jerusalem, God unfolds his story in places of importance. To God, place matters.

By comparison, place is trivial for most of us. In our highly mobile and globalized world, we see the whole world as our place. Unfortunately, a highly mobile and transient lifestyle does not allow for the development of deeper relationships in our families or communities. While technological communication has attempted to move into the gap, it is a poor substitute for slower face to face communication. As we age, it is important that we give serious consideration to the place or places where we will age.

Numerous surveys have shown that the vast majority of older adults would prefer to age in place in their current home. As a result, we are seeing the development of technologies and businesses that will make aging in place more feasible for older adults. In addition, this movement affords an excellent opportunity for churches and the Christian community to develop ministries that will both serve an aging population and empower older adults to serve. Christians can show the love of Jesus Christ in tangible ways by using their gifts, abilities, and resources in serving older adults who are aging in place.

A theology of place is also important. You are not in your current place by accident. God has you there for his purposes. God wants you to bring his love to the place he has for you. What relationships does God want you to nurture and grow? What about your friends? What about your kids and grandkids? What about your aging parents?

Now is the time for us to think creatively about aging in place...both for ourselves and for the people God brings to us. By 2020 there will be about 74 million Americans over the age of 60. How does God want to use you in the place where he plants you? It's time for followers of Jesus Christ to learn what God wants us to do as we age in place.

YOUR TAKE

Answer the questions that follow. Discuss your responses with your group.

1. As you think about aging, where do you want to live in your final years?

___ I want to live independently in my own home.

___ I want to live with my children or other relatives.

___ I want to live in an assisted living community.

___ I want to live in a 55+ community and stay active.

___ I want to live on a golf course.

___ I want to live on the coast.

___ I want to live in the desert.

___ I want to live in another country.

___ I want to live in a nursing home.

___ I want to live in a RV.

___ I want to live in subsidized housing.

__ I want to live in a communal setting.

__ Other _____.

2. When you think of aging in place, which of the following issues concern you the most?

__ Enough income	__ Home repairs
__ Physical safety	__ Social life
__ Health care	__ Shopping
__ Transportation	__ Memory loss
__ Loneliness	__ Mobility
__ Recreation	__ Other _____

YOUR REFLECTION

Read the following passages from the Bible and answer the questions that follow.

This is what the LORD Almighty, the God of Israel, says to all those I carried into exile from Jerusalem to Babylon: "Build houses and settle down; plant gardens and eat what they produce. Marry and have sons and daughters; find wives for your sons and give your daughters in marriage, so that they too may have sons and daughters. Increase in number there; do not decrease. Also, seek the peace and prosperity of the city to which I have carried you into exile. Pray to the LORD for it, because if it prospers, you too will prosper."
—Jeremiah 29: 4-7

1. Why did God tell the Israelite exiles to settle into Babylon?

2. What relevance does this message have for us as we consider aging in place?

When Jesus saw the crowd around him, he gave orders to cross to the other side of the lake. Then a teacher of the law came to him and said, "Teacher, I will follow you wherever you go."

Jesus replied, "Foxes have dens and birds have nests, but the Son of Man has no place to lay his head."

Another disciple said to him, "Lord, first let me go and bury my father."

But Jesus told him, "Follow me, and let the dead bury their own dead."
—Matthew 8:18-22

3. Is Jesus minimizing the important of place in these verses? Please explain your response.

4. If Jesus said these words to you, how do you think you would respond?

"Do not let your hearts be troubled. You believe in God; believe also in me. My Father's house has many rooms; if that were not so, would I have told you that I am going there to prepare a place for you? And if I

go and prepare a place for you, I will come back and take you to be with me that you also may be where I am. You know the way to the place where I am going."
—John 14:1-4

5. As you age, have you had trouble finding a place of comfort and rest? If so, what is troubling you and how are you dealing with it?

6. What is our ultimate place of rest and how do we get there?

YOUR APPLICATION
During the coming week think about and reflect on the following.

1. Most of us will have a place or places where we age. Whatever place we choose, we need to make it a sacred place. As you think about the place or places you will age, spend some time reflecting on these following quotes.

"There is always in life a place to leave and a new place to find, and in between a zone of hesitation and uncertainty tinged with more or less intense anxiety."
—Paul Tournier, A Place for You

"Home is the place where, when you have to go there, they have to take you in."
—Robert Frost

"If a man cannot be a Christian in the place he is, he cannot be a Christian anywhere."
—Henry Ward Beecher

"My home is in Heaven. I'm just traveling through this world."
—Billy Graham

"Home is where the heart is."
—Pliny the Elder

2. Spend some time this week reflecting on Jesus' words in these verses and write down your thoughts.

"When Jesus saw the crowd around him, he gave orders to cross to the other side of the lake. Then a teacher of the law came to him and said, "Teacher, I will follow you wherever you go."

Jesus replied, "Foxes have dens and birds have nests, but the Son of Man has no place to lay his head."

Another disciple said to him, "Lord, first let me go and bury my father."

But Jesus told him, "Follow me, and let the dead bury their own dead."
—Matthew 8:18-22

"Do not let your hearts be troubled. You believe in God; believe also in me. My Father's house has many rooms; if that were not so, would I have told you that I am going there to prepare a place for you? And if I go and prepare a place for you, I will come back and take you to be with me that you also may be where I am. You know the way to the place where I am going."
—John 14:1-4

SESSION 5 | SPIRITUAL STRENGTH

INTRODUCTION
Have one or more group members read the introduction aloud.

The Issue: How can we strengthen ourselves spiritually as we age?

In his book *Nearing Home*, Billy Graham writes, "'Golden years' must have been coined by the young. It is doubtful that anyone over seventy would have described this phase of life with such a symbolic word." As we get older, many of us agree with his sentiments. Our bodies remind us often that we are no longer in our 20s, 30s, or even 40s. Now getting out of bed in the morning seems to come at such an inconvenient time.

Life has a way of beating us up. As we grow older not only does the wear and tear of life cause the loss of physical strength, but we may also see our spiritual strength wane. But there are many passages in the Bible that encourage and exhort us to maintain and grow our spiritual presence. Certainly, retaining and growing their spiritual strength was the challenge of many biblical characters. We read that "David was greatly distressed, for the people spoke of stoning him, because all the people were bitter in soul, each for his sons and daughters. But David strengthened himself in the Lord his God." The apostle Paul writes that "the Lord stood by me and strengthened me, so that through me the message might be fully proclaimed and all the Gentiles might hear it. So I was rescued from the lion's mouth." And Peter reminds us in scripture that "whoever speaks, as one who speaks oracles of God; whoever serves, as one who serves by the strength that God supplies—in order that in everything God may be glorified through Jesus Christ. To him belong glory and dominion forever and ever. Amen."

As we age, our spiritual strength should grow and deepen. The Bible makes it clear that spiritual strength comes from God. For example, in Isaiah we read, "do not fear, for I am with you; do not be dismayed, for I am your God. I will strengthen you and help you; I will uphold you with my righteous right hand." As God strengthens us, he gives us wisdom and understanding into his ways. The book of Proverbs emphatically instructs us to seek God's wisdom and understanding and put them into use, especially in guiding younger generations.

As we grow older, the strength and wisdom of God is manifested as Christ-like behavior in our lives. With God's strength, we are transformed into people who would live out his wisdom over and against the wisdom of the world. The book of James contrasts these two wisdoms for us: *Who is wise and understanding among you? Let them show it by their good life, by deeds done in the humility that comes from wisdom. But if you harbor bitter envy and selfish ambition in your hearts, do not boast about it or deny the truth. Such "wisdom" does not come down from heaven but is earthly, unspiritual, demonic. For where you have envy and selfish ambition, there you find disorder and every evil practice. But the wisdom that comes from heaven is first of all pure; then peace-loving, considerate, submissive, full of mercy and good fruit, impartial and sincere. Peacemakers who sow in peace reap a harvest of righteousness.*

We cannot live and look like Jesus through our own power and strength. We are dependent on the Holy Spirit to change us. Such spiritual transformation should go deeper as we age. Certainly, God is not done with us, no matter our age. Let us be willing to let God strengthen us and continue his work in and through us.

YOUR TAKE

Answer the questions that follow. Discuss your responses with your group.

1. On a scale of 1 to 10, where 1 = no spiritual strength and 10 = walking in unison with the Holy Spirit, how would you rate your spiritual strength?

| 1 | 2 | 3 | 4 | 5 | 6 | 7 | 8 | 9 | 10 |

2. What would it take for you to strengthen your spiritual life? What practical steps do you need to take to make spiritual strengthening a reality?

YOUR REFLECTION
Read the following passages from the Bible and answer the questions that follow.

Have you not known? Have you not heard? The LORD is the everlasting God, the Creator of the ends of the earth. He does not faint or grow weary; his understanding is unsearchable. He gives power to the faint, and to him who has no might he increases strength. Even youths shall faint and be weary, and young men shall fall exhausted; but they who wait for the Lord shall renew their strength; they shall mount up with wings like eagles; they shall run and not be weary; they shall walk and not faint.
—Isaiah 40:28-31

1. Why is it important that God not grow weary or tired?

2. If God's "understanding is unsearchable," how do we gain wisdom and understanding?

3. What does it mean to "wait for the Lord?" How has God strengthened you over the years?

We are hard pressed on every side, but not crushed; perplexed, but not in despair; persecuted, but not abandoned; struck down, but not destroyed. We always carry around in our body the death of Jesus, so that the life of Jesus may also be revealed in our body. For we who are alive are always being given over to death for Jesus' sake, so that his life may also be revealed in our mortal body. So then, death is at work in us, but life is at work in you.

It is written: "I believed; therefore I have spoken." Since we have that same spirit of faith, we also believe and therefore speak, because we know that the one who raised the Lord Jesus from the dead will also raise us with Jesus and present us with you to himself. All this is for your benefit, so that the grace that is reaching more and more people may cause thanksgiving to overflow to the glory of God.

Therefore we do not lose heart. Though outwardly we are wasting away, yet inwardly we are being renewed day by day. For our light and momentary troubles are achieving for us an eternal glory that far outweighs them all. So we fix our eyes not on what is seen, but on what is unseen, since what is seen is temporary, but what is unseen is eternal.
—*2 Corinthians 4:8-18*

4. After his conversion, the apostle Paul dealt with much physical, emotional, and spiritual trauma. How was he able to keep on going?

5. In what ways was Paul "a dead man walking?"

6. What does it mean to be outwardly wasting away and, at the same time, being renewed? How does an eternal perspective affect how well we do in this life?

YOUR APPLICATION

During the coming week meditate and reflect on the following verses and quotes. Write down the thoughts and reflections these verses and quotes may produce.

Bible Verses:

"Look to the Lord and his strength, seek his face always."
—1 Chronicles 16:11

"The LORD is my strength and my defense; he has become my salvation. He is my God, and I will praise him, my father's God, and I will exalt him."
—Exodus 15:2

"I can do all this through him who gives me strength."
—Philippians 4:13

"The Lord is my light and my salvation--whom shall I fear? The Lord is the stronghold of my life--of whom shall I be afraid?"
—Psalm 27:1

"Be strong and courageous. Do not be afraid or terrified because of them, for the LORD your God goes with you; he will never leave you nor forsake you."
—Deuteronomy 31:6

"I have told you these things, so that in me you may have peace. In this world you will have trouble. But take heart! I have overcome the world."
—John 16:33

Therefore we do not lose heart. Though outwardly we are wasting away, yet inwardly we are being renewed day by day. For our light and momentary troubles are achieving for us an eternal glory that far outweighs them all. So we fix our eyes not on what is seen, but on what is unseen, since what is seen is temporary, but what is unseen is eternal.
—2 Corinthians 4:16-18

Quotes:
"I think God has planned the strength and beauty of youth to be physical. But the strength and beauty of old age is spiritual. We gradually lose the strength and beauty that is temporary so we'll be sure to concentrate on the strength and beauty that is forever."
— J. Robertson McQuilkin

"Autumn is really the best of the seasons; and I'm not sure that old age isn't the best part of life. But, of course, like Autumn, it doesn't last!"
—C. S. Lewis

"The more sand that has escaped from the hourglass of our life, the clearer we should see through it."
—Jean Paul

"Do not look forward to what may happen tomorrow; the same everlasting Father who cares for you today will take care of you tomorrow and every day. Either He will shield you from suffering, or He will give you unfailing strength to bear it."
—St. Francis de Sales

SESSION 6 | KNOCKIN' ON HEAVEN'S DOOR

INTRODUCTION
Have one or more group members read the introduction aloud.

The Issue: What will your attitude be as you come to the end of your life?

Ben Franklin is quoted as saying, "In this world nothing can be said to be certain, except death and taxes." Years later, Will Rogers responded with "The only difference between death and taxes is that death doesn't get worse every time Congress meets." We often make jokes about death because we are uncomfortable with it. Perhaps our response to death is similar to Woody Allen's when he said, "I am not afraid of death; I just don't want to be there when it happens."

Despite our discomfort or denial of death, it is a stark reality for all of us. None of us will get out of this life alive. While death is not what God intended when he created mankind, it need not be a subject we avoid or dismiss. In fact, comprehending and apprehending the reality of death--especially our death--can bring life into greater focus. There is a line from the song *The Rose* that succinctly captures this thought: "The soul afraid of dying that never learns to live."

Again, death has a way of bringing life into clearer focus. It's amazing how interested people become in the meaning of life when they attend a funeral or memorial service. Unfortunately, this interest usually fades in a few days. Busyness, denial, fear, and many other distractions keep us from reflecting on the meaning of life in the face of death. Yet, Socrates is still right today as when he wrote that "the unexamined life is not worth living."

For followers of Jesus Christ, there is no reason to deny or fear death. Jesus came and defeated sin and death; and through him, we can too. This is the central message of the gospel, the good news. *"For God so loved the world that he gave his one and only Son, that whoever believes in him shall not perish but have eternal life. For God did not send his Son into the world to condemn the world, but to save the world through him"* (John 3:16-17) Facing death without the hope of the gospel and the promise of eternal life is a woeful place to be.

As we age and get closer to death, we have an opportunity to deepen our relationship with God. The reality of death should help us focus on the spiritual side of our human existence. The Bible makes it clear that we have a spiritual life as well as a physical life. When we allow the Holy Spirit to transform us, visible changes take place, the fruit of the Spirit results. *"The fruit of the Spirit is love, joy, peace, forbearance, kindness, goodness, faithfulness, gentleness and self-control."* (Galatians 5:22, 23)

Even in the face of death, the message for Christ followers is clear. While loving God, we are to show the love of Christ to our family, friends, neighbors, and all we meet. Jesus put it succinctly when he said, *"'Love the Lord your God with all your heart and with all your soul and with all your mind. 'This is the first and greatest commandment. And the second is like it: 'Love your neighbor as yourself.'"* We are called to be lovers of God and others until we die. God is not done with any of us here on earth until he calls us home.

YOUR TAKE
Answer the questions that follow. Discuss your responses with your group.

1. Which of the following statements best describes your attitude toward death and dying?

___ I don't want to think about it.

___ I don't fear death, but I do fear suffering.

___ I agree with Woody Allen, I don't fear death. I just don't want to be there when it happens.

___ Death is a reality of life; accept it.

___ Death is not the end, but the beginning of a new and better life.

___ I would welcome death since I am tired of this life.

___ Death is a mystery and so is life.

___ I don't fear death, but I will miss my loved ones.

___ Other _____.

2. In her book On Death and Dying, Dr. Elisabeth Kübler-Ross identified 5 stages of grief as one faces death. In your experience with dying people, which of these stages have you observed and how did the dying person react?

___ **Denial** *"I feel fine." "This can't be happening, not to me."*

___ **Anger** *"Why me? It's not fair!" "How can it happen to me; who's to blame?"*

___ **Bargaining** *"I'll do anything for a few more years." "God, what do you want me to do?*

___ **Depression** *"I'm so sad, why bother with anything?"; "I'm going to die soon so what's the point?"*

___ **Acceptance** *"It's going to be okay."; "I can't fight it, I may as well prepare for it."*

YOUR REFLECTION

Read the following passages from the Bible and answer the questions that follow.

Then Jesus went with his disciples to a place called Gethsemane, and he said to them, "Sit here while I go over there and pray." He took Peter and the two sons of Zebedee along with him, and he began to be sorrowful and troubled. Then he said to them, "My soul is overwhelmed with sorrow to the point of death. Stay here and keep watch with me."

Going a little farther, he fell with his face to the ground and prayed, "My Father, if it is possible, may this cup be taken from me. Yet not as I will, but as you will."

Then he returned to his disciples and found them sleeping. "Couldn't you men keep watch with me for one hour?" he asked Peter. "Watch and pray so that you will not fall into temptation. The spirit is willing, but the flesh is weak."

He went away a second time and prayed, "My Father, if it is not possible for this cup to be taken away unless I drink it, may your will be done."

When he came back, he again found them sleeping, because their eyes were heavy. So he left them and went away once more and prayed the third time, saying the same thing.

Then he returned to the disciples and said to them, "Are you still sleeping and resting? Look, the hour has come, and the Son of Man is delivered into the hands of sinners. Rise! Let us go! Here comes my betrayer!"
—Matthew 26:36-46

1. As Jesus faced his death on the cross, what stages of grief does he exhibit in this passage?

2. Why was Jesus Christ so overcome with grief here?

3. When confronted with suffering and death, how is our behavior similar to that of the disciples?

I declare to you, brothers and sisters, that flesh and blood cannot inherit the kingdom of God, nor does the perishable inherit the imperishable. Listen, I tell you a mystery: We will not all sleep, but we will all be changed—in a flash, in the twinkling of an eye, at the last trumpet. For the trumpet will sound, the dead will be raised imperishable, and we will be changed. For the perishable must clothe itself with the imperishable, and the mortal with immortality. When the perishable has been clothed with the imperishable, and the mortal with immortality, then the saying that is written will come true: "Death has been swallowed up in victory."

"Where, O death, is your victory? Where, O death, is your sting?"

The sting of death is sin, and the power of sin is the law. But thanks be to God! He gives us the victory through our Lord Jesus Christ.

Therefore, my dear brothers and sisters, stand firm. Let nothing move you. Always give yourselves fully to the work of the Lord, because you know that your labor in the Lord is not in vain.
—1 Corinthians 15:50-58

4. Do you believe that humans can be immortal? What does immortality mean to you?

5. For followers of Jesus Christ, why does death not have any victory? Why does death not produce a sting?

6. Ultimately, for Christ followers, what does it mean to finish well?

YOUR APPLICATION

During the coming week meditate and reflect on the following questions. Write down your thoughts and reflections as you respond to these questions.

1. How much have you thought about your own death? How does it make you feel when you think about it?

2. Have you prepared, in any way, for your death? Reflect on the following questions.

a. Who would you want to tell that you loved them—and why?

b. To whom would you want to apologize?

c. Do you need to talk to God about some important issues?

d. Are there any messages that need to be communicated to family, friends, or others that you have not expressed?

e. What advice would you give to your loved ones?

f. Are there any contributions or donations you need to make?

g. If you only had a month to live, how would you spend that time?

FURTHER READING

Choosing to See: A Journey of Struggle and Hope by Mary Beth Chapman

A Grief Observed by C. S. Lewis

On Death and Dying by Elisabeth Kubler-Ross

Good Grief by Granger E. Westberg

Walking with God through Pain and Suffering by Timothy Keller

Experiencing Grief by H. Norman Wright

ABOUT THE AUTHOR

Peter Menconi has written and presented widely on generational and aging issues. His rich background as a dentist, pastor, counselor, business owner, conference speaker, husband, father, and grandfather brings unique perspectives to his writing.

Born and raised in Chicago, Pete graduated from the University of Illinois, College of Dentistry and practiced dentistry for 23 years in private practice, in the U.S. Army and in a mission hospital in Kenya, East Africa. In addition, Pete has a M.S. in Counseling Psychology and several years of seminary training. He has also been a commodity futures floor trader, a speaker with the American Dental Association, and a broker of medical and dental practices.

For over 20 years Pete was the outreach pastor at a large church in suburban Denver, Colorado. Currently, he is the president of Mt. Sage Publishing and board member with the CASA Network.

Pete's writings include the book *The Intergenerational Church: Understanding Congregations from WWII to www.com*, The Support Group Series, a 9-book Bible study series, and numerous articles.

Pete and his wife Jean live in the Denver area and they are the parents of 3 adult children and the grandparents of 9 grandchildren.

Pete Menconi can be reached at petermenconi@msn.com.

CASA NETWORK

AGING WELL

BIBLESTUDY**SERIES**

Finally, a Bible study series for everyone 50 and over
who wants to stay in the game as long as possible!

THE AGING CHALLENGE

The primary purpose of this Bible study is to
help you take a fresh look at aging, reevaluate
your current situation, and consider making
some changes.

THE NEW R & R: RETIRED AND REWIRED

The primary purpose of this Bible study is to
help you to take a fresh look at retirement,
reevaluate your current situation, and consider
making some changes.

GENERATIONS TOGETHER

The primary purpose of this Bible study is to
help you to take a fresh look at our current
generations, how the generations relate, and
how we can be better together.

Available at www.Amazon.com

SAGE OR CURMUDGEON

The primary purpose of this Bible study is to help you to take a closer look at your attitude about aging, how to reevaluate your attitude, and how to move toward becoming a sage for younger people.

THE AGING FAMILY AND MARRIAGE

The primary purpose of this Bible study is to help you to take a closer look at your aging marriage and/or family and see how you can maximize these relationships.

FINISHING WELL

The primary purpose of this Bible study is to help you to take a closer look at how you can finish well before your life is over.

Available at www.Amazon.com

THE INTERGENERATIONAL CHURCH:
Understanding Congregations from
WWII to www.com

Are certain generations underrepresented in your church?

Would you like to see more young adults in your congregation?

The Intergenerational Church: Understanding Congregations from WWII to www.com will show you why understanding today's generations is crucial for the survival and thrival of the local church.

The Intergenerational Church is a breakthrough book that will help you meet the Intergenerational Challenge.

FROM THIS IMPORTANT BOOK, YOU WILL LEARN HOW TO:

- Minimize generational tension.
- Get all the generations moving in the same direction.
- Develop leaders from all generations.
- Deliver intergenerational preaching.
- Cultivate intergenerational worship and community.
- Stimulate intergenerational mission and outreach.

Made in the USA
Lexington, KY
30 January 2015